PURNELL'S **LIFE CYCLE** BOOK OF
cats

Written by Ronald Ridout and Michael Holt
Illustrated by Tony Payne

About the Authors

RONALD RIDOUT'S name appears on almost 46 million educational books. He is the "world's best selling educational writer" (*Guinness Book of Records*). A famous pioneer in the field of education, he believes that children "should get the meaning off the page".

He has published 277 books mainly educational. After gaining his diploma at Oxford University he taught for seven years, joined an educational publishing company and eventually turned to full-time writing and editing of books.

Ronald Ridout now works from his home in Haslemere and his books sell some 2½ million copies each year.

MICHAEL HOLT has been an actor, a research physicist, an editor and a senior lecturer in mathematics.

He is now a freelance writer with a deep interest in how children learn and has written many highly successful textbooks.

Michael Holt is married with two children and lives in Herefordshire where he studies snakes, toads and frogs.

First published 1974 by Purnell Books
Second Impression 1975
Text copyright © 1974 RR Productions
    Limited and Michael Holt
Illustrations copyright © 1974 Purnell &
    Sons Limited

Designed and produced for Purnell Books by
ibp Intercontinental Book Productions

Printed in Yugoslavia
SBN 361 02783 4

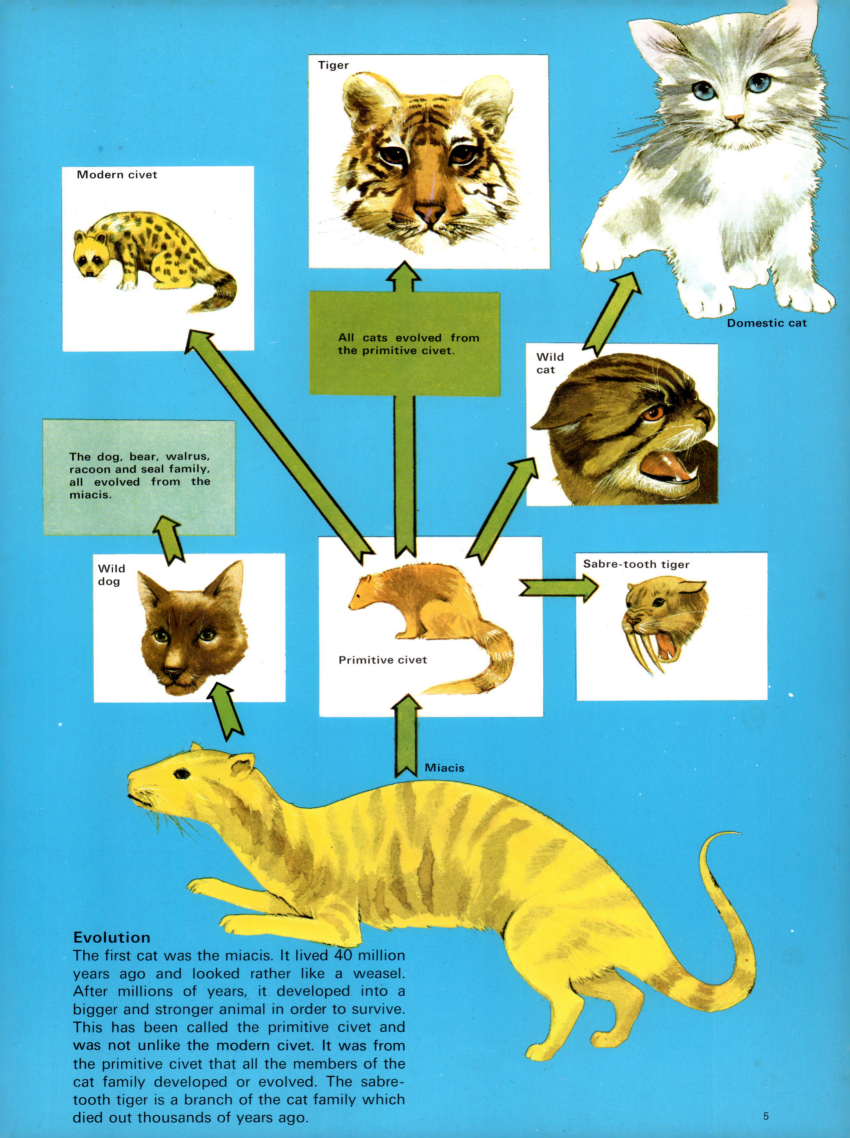

Modern civet

Tiger

Domestic cat

All cats evolved from the primitive civet.

Wild cat

The dog, bear, walrus, racoon and seal family, all evolved from the miacis.

Wild dog

Primitive civet

Sabre-tooth tiger

Miacis

Evolution

The first cat was the miacis. It lived 40 million years ago and looked rather like a weasel. After millions of years, it developed into a bigger and stronger animal in order to survive. This has been called the primitive civet and was not unlike the modern civet. It was from the primitive civet that all the members of the cat family developed or evolved. The sabre-tooth tiger is a branch of the cat family which died out thousands of years ago.

The cat family

The cat family includes many species or kinds. The best known are the lion, tiger, leopard, cheetah, jaguar, lynx, wild cat and domestic cat. All these species are alike in many ways. To help them move quietly while they are hunting, they all walk on cushioned pads that are their toes. They are all quick off the mark and can climb trees and rocks. They are carnivores (meat-eaters) and have sharp claws and teeth to tear the meat. All of them have whiskers to feel with. They *purr* and have a good sense of smell. As well as all these things, they all have keen sight, even in dim light.

Above: The sabre-tooth tiger lived 100,000 years ago. There are none alive today. The modern cat family has existed for several million years and has remained much the same except that the various sabre-tooth tigers have died out, though no one knows why.

Left: The cheetah is the fastest cat. It can accelerate to 75 kph in 2 seconds and can reach a speed of 105 kph for about 300 metres, though it cannot keep up this speed for longer. A race-horse would be able to overtake it after about 400 metres.

This domestic short-hair cat, known as a tabby, is the original domestic cat, and is still the most common of all pet cats.

This is a wild cat, called the Desert Cat of India. A wild cat can often be tamed but never domesticated; the kittens of a wild cat are always wild and have to be tamed. The kittens of the domestic cat do not have to be tamed.

The lion is the largest member of the cat family. Some male lions are more than 3 metres from nose to tail. The lion is the only cat that is not a complete 'loner'. Lions may hunt together and live in groups, called prides.

The Ancient Egyptians were the first known people to have domestic cats. They believed they had some blood kinship with cats and so they worshipped statues of them, called totems. Below is a drawing of one of their totems. In time the totem cat became a god. The cat-headed god was called *Pasht*. From this name we get the word 'puss'.

Cat history

The domestic cat that we keep as a pet today almost certainly evolved from the wild species. It is not, however, just a tamed wild cat. Wild cats, however much they are tamed, still breed *wild* cats.

It took thousands of years for certain wild cats, cut off from the rest, to turn into domestic cats. Each new litter of these tamed wild cats must have become a little less wild than the last, till thousands of years later they became a new species—domestic cats that had tame kittens. At any rate, it is known for certain that domestic cats already existed 4,000 or so years ago in Ancient Egypt.

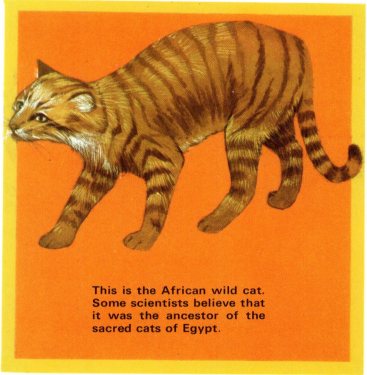

This is the African wild cat. Some scientists believe that it was the ancestor of the sacred cats of Egypt.

Another wild cat, the Golden Cat of Africa.

The European Wild Cat looks rather like the domestic tabby cat. Our domestic cats have probably descended from a mixture of wild cats.

The Pallas cat lives in rocky country between the Caspian Sea and Mongolia. People used to think that the modern Persian cat was descended from it. Scientists now think this unlikely.

The wild cat probably came into the house of early man for food and warmth. They were welcomed because they killed rats and mice. Perhaps the children tamed some of them. There were kittens and they tamed these too. This went on for thousands of years till a new breed of cat appeared—the domestic cat.

A long-haired Tortoiseshell-and-White.

Breeding

From the first known domestic cats of Ancient Egypt till quite recently, our pet cats were all tabbies. Then about a hundred years ago people started to breed cats to get a special colour or length of hair. From each litter of tabbies, they chose the one most like the cat they wanted to develop and bred from that one. From that cat's litter they chose the best cat again. From the next litter, they selected once more. From this selective breeding over many years, they finally produced a new pure breed that would go on producing pure-bred kittens.

1. Many people believe that the Abyssinian cat is a direct descendant of the sacred Egyptian cats but this legend is not taken seriously by scientists.

2. The Siamese cat was one of the first pure breeds. Its name is part of another legend. There is no evidence that it came from Siam.

3. A legend tells that the Birman cat came from the temples of Burma. It is now known that it was bred selectively in France from tabbies.

4. The Blue Persian is handsome, quiet and gentle. It is perhaps the most popular of the long-haired breeds.

A FEMALE CAT

Here we can see where the reproductive organs are located in a female cat.

Reproduction

Every cat begins life as an egg. At first the egg is a tiny speck inside the female (queen) cat. It cannot grow into an animal by itself. It must be joined by sperm from a male cat. Then it

Below: The diagram shows the internal reproductive organs of the female cat. These are used in the making of the eggs and finally the unborn kitten.

1. Ovaries, where the eggs are made

2. Tube, along which the eggs and sperm travel

3. Vagina

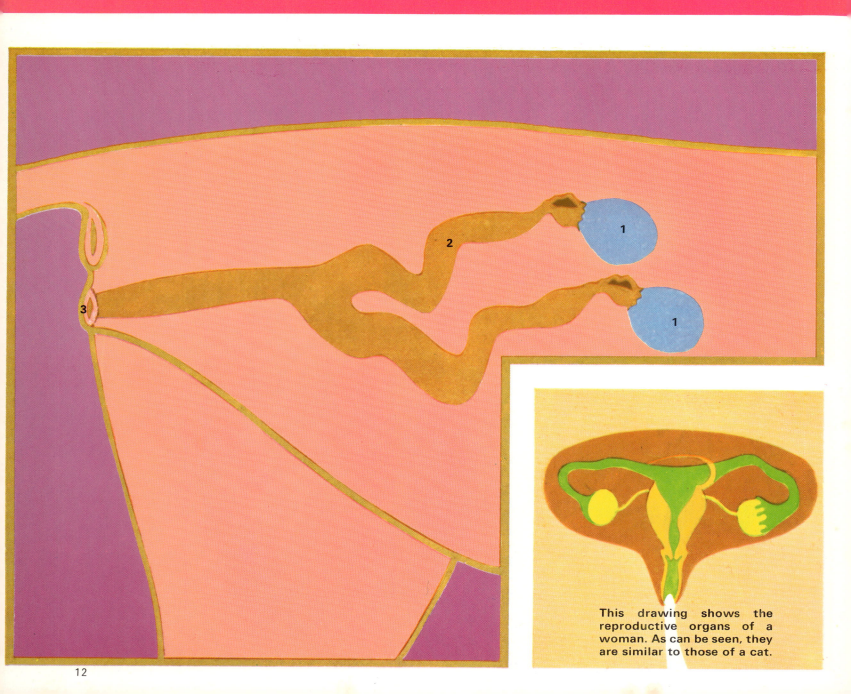

This drawing shows the reproductive organs of a woman. As can be seen, they are similar to those of a cat.

will start growing into a new animal. The female cat makes eggs inside her body. The male cat makes sperm inside his body. The sperm joins the eggs to fertilise them when the male and female cats mate.

Below: This diagram shows the reproductive organs of the male cat. It is with these organs that the sperm is made and transferred to the female.

1. Anus

2. Testes, where the sperm is made

3. Penis

4. Spermatic cords, along which the sperm travels

5. Bladder

A MALE CAT

Here we can see where the reproductive organs are located in a male cat.

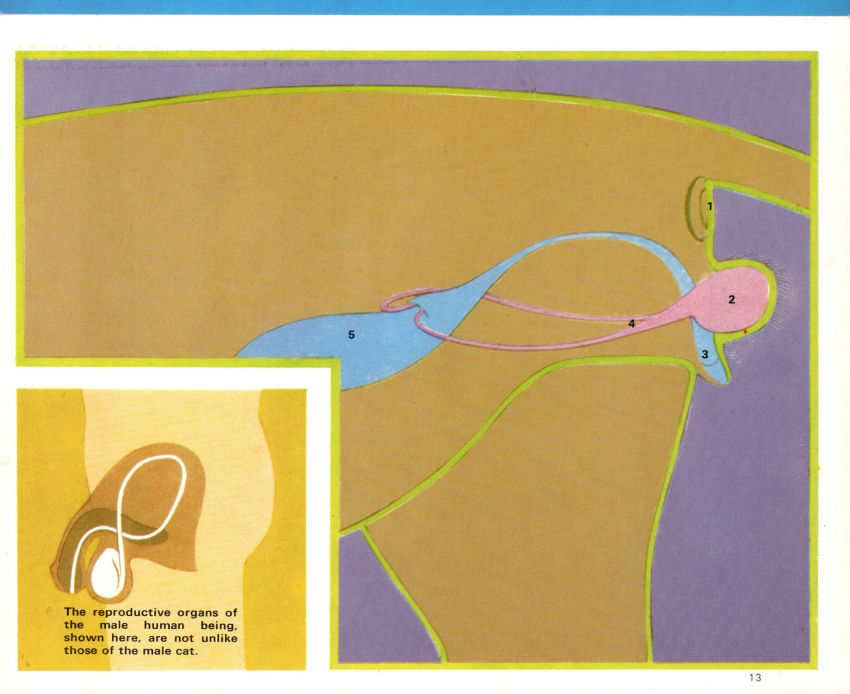

The reproductive organs of the male human being, shown here, are not unlike those of the male cat.

The female cat rolls on the ground in front of the male during courtship.

A female cat (above) makes the mating call which will help attract the male to her.

Mating

The male cat finds the female by instinct. He is partly guided by the female's mating call but he is more certainly guided by the scent of the female 'on heat'. The queen is not ready to mate until she comes on heat. You can usually tell when a cat is on heat by the way she rolls about on the floor and rubs herself lovingly against people's legs.

The courtship does not last long. The male caterwauls to the female. She rubs her nose and mouth against objects and then rolls in front of the male. Finally she crouches ready to be mounted.

The male climbs upon her back, gripping her firmly by the back of the neck. In this position his penis can enter the vagina of the female cat. This is known as mating. The sperm from his penis enters the vagina and flows up the tube to the eggs.

Above: The male mounts the female and inserts his penis in her vagina to allow his sperm to reach the eggs.

Left: An enlarged illustration of the male cat's penis in the female's vagina.

Fertilisation

The female cat's eggs leave the ovary and travel down a tube to the uterus. It is here that they are fertilised by the sperm from the male cat.

Inside each tiny egg there is now a new life growing. At this stage it is known as an embryo. It is here in the uterus that the embryos gradually grow into kittens. At each stage of growth the embryos become more like real kittens, till, after about 63 days, they are ready to be born.

Above left: Enlargement of an egg of a female cat. It shows the sperm about to enter it. When the sperm has entered, the egg becomes fertilised and can begin growing into a new cat. No other sperm can now enter the egg. The female cat may have more than one mate, but it is usually the first one that fertilises the eggs.
Above right: The egg divides into 2 cells and then into 4 cells, and so on, until there are hundreds of cells.

1. After about ten days the hundreds of tiny cells begin to form a shape in which we can just recognise the head.

2. By two weeks, the head, eye and tail are clearly visible; and so is the umbilical cord that attaches the embryo to the uterus.

3. After nine weeks, the limbs begin to form. The front legs can be clearly seen, though the hind legs are still the merest buds.

4. A little later, both pairs of legs are much clearer, and the tail looks more like a cat's tail. The embryo is still being fed through the umbilical cord.

5. By 35 days the ears become visible, and the legs have recognisable feet and claws.

6. After 45 days the foetus is fully formed and will now go on growing till ready to be born after about 63 days.

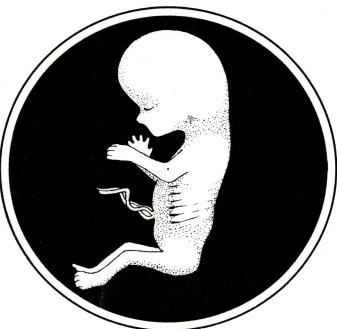

Above: Human foetus at 60 days. The human foetus still has another 7 months in which to develop and grow.

Left: Cat foetus at 60 days. The cat is almost ready to be born.

The growing foetus

From the time the eggs are fertilised to the time the kittens are born averages 63 days. By comparison, some butterfly eggs in hot countries turn into caterpillars in 5 or 6 days. A hen's eggs take around 21 days to turn into chicks. The human egg will take about 280 days to turn into a baby. But though the length of time varies from creature to creature, all embryos look rather alike after a quarter of the time has passed. Scientists believe that this is evidence of evolution—an indication that higher animals have developed from lower ones. In the end, of course, all embryos grow into completely different creatures.

Below: A female cat giving birth to one of her kittens. The circular cut-away drawing shows a kitten being born and other kittens of the litter waiting to emerge.

The birth

As the 63 days come near an end, the cat becomes interested in snug corners. She is looking for a quiet place to have her kittens. It is usually well away from everyone in a rather dark place, and here she makes her nest. At this time she becomes very restless, miaows a great deal and demands a lot of attention. Then she will disappear altogether into her nest for a long spell.

When a kitten is ready to be born, the mother cat contracts her stomach muscles and squeezes. She does this several times, pushing the unborn baby down the uterus towards the enlarged vagina. Presently the head of the kitten appears through the vagina and a moment later the whole kitten appears. Each kitten is born one at a time in this way. The average number of kittens in a litter is 4 and there may be 20 minutes to an hour between each birth.

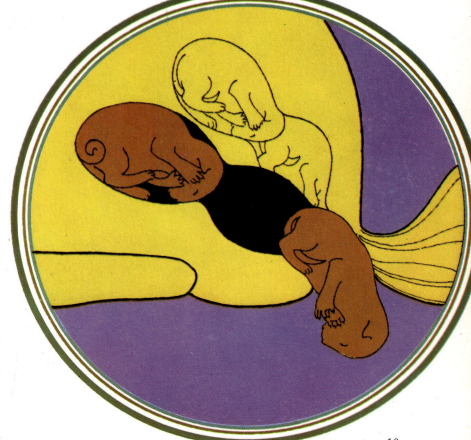

When the kitten is born the cat cuts the umbilical cord with her teeth.

The cat licks her new born kittens to clean them and stimulate their nervous systems.

After the birth

Usually the kitten is born in a sac of tissue, called the placenta, in which it 'floated' inside its mother. The mother cat cuts this with her teeth and then licks the kittens clean. The mother cat licks the new born kitten very vigorously, not just to clean it, but also to stimulate the nervous system.

At birth the kitten is still attached to its mother by the umbilical cord. As she licks the kitten, the cat finds this cord and severs it with her teeth. She swallows this with the placenta.

The top picture shows the mother cat cradling her young kittens so that they can take milk from her nipples. Below right is a close-up of a kitten suckling.

Suckling

New born kittens are very small—not much bigger than mice—and they cannot see. In spite of this, each kitten will find a nipple to take milk from its mother. At first the mother will circle her kittens with her legs and cradle them towards her nipples. But after a few hours the kittens are able to suckle unaided, guided by their sense of smell. When they are not suckling, they go to sleep.

The first few days

At first the mother cat looks after her kittens very carefully and will let no stranger come near them. When she leaves the nest, the kittens huddle together for warmth. After 5 to 10 days they open their eyes. By this time they can just stand up and crawl and they are growing fast. Soon they are able to walk about in the nest and grab or make little pounces.

While their mother is away these kittens look for mischief.

If a nursing cat is interfered with or in any way frightened, she may decide to find a new nesting place. She then picks up each kitten by the scruff of the neck and carries it to the new place. This does not hurt the kitten. Cats can 'count'; the mother cat knows when she has taken all her litter.

Below: This kitten is 8 days old and has opened its eyes for the first time. All kittens' eyes are blue at first.

Handling young kittens

By about the 15th day, the boldest kitten will climb out of the nest and take a few steps outside. Within a few days all the kittens will be venturing out. They will take a dozen or so steps then rush back to the safety of their mother.

At this stage they can be picked up. To do this, place a hand, palm upwards, on the floor and wriggle the fingers at the kittens. One of them will come and sniff them. Stroke the kitten's head with a finger and when the kitten begins to purr contentedly, it can be picked up.

This kitten is going to pounce on the ball. It is playing at hunting. Kittens don't realise this, but their play is teaching them to hunt when they are grown up.

Lessons from the mother cat

As soon as the kittens have left the nest, the mother cat will start teaching them how to keep their claws sharp; she will help them to become house-trained and she will teach them by playing lots of different games. So, it is by their mother's example that the kittens learn the many things they need to know to become fine, healthy and bright cats.

This kitten is practising crawling in a crouched position, as if hiding in long grass while getting near its prey.

Kittens have to learn to hunt. After the play stage, they are given their first taste of the real thing. The mother cat brings them a half-killed mouse.

The bones of a cat's foot show the claw extended (top) and withdrawn (bottom).

A cat's claws are kept sharp by scratching. Here is a kitten using a scratching post for this purpose.

A cat has 5 claws on each fore paw and 4 on each hind paw. It can draw in its claws when they are not needed, as in the paw on the left. It also draws them in when 'pretend' fighting.

Cats are clean animals. In their wild state they dig a hole and cover their droppings by scratching earth over them. Instinct tells them to do this. The domestic cat also teaches her young to cover its droppings even in a sand tray provided by the owner.

Growing up

As the kittens grow up, the mother cat spends less time with them. They gradually take less milk from her and she shows them how to lap milk from a saucer. At five weeks they are eating solid food too.

Soon after that, their mother will bring them their first mouse. A few days later they will be following her on their first real hunting trip.

At about 8 weeks they stop taking milk from their mother and feed themselves.

1. Mother watches her kitten as it takes its first licks at a saucer of milk.

2. Close-up of a cat's tongue showing the rough *papillae* which enable the cat to clean itself and lick a bone clean.

3. This 5 week-old kitten is licking itself. Kittens have to learn to lick themselves clean especially after eating. At first the mother cat regularly licks her kittens clean. Later on she teaches her kittens how to do it themselves.

Though it is difficult to make cats do tricks, they learn to perform many complicated actions at their own wish. This cat taught herself to press the latch of the back door and let herself into the house.

By watching people, cats seem to learn the most surprising things. This one learned to ring the front door-bell to be let in. Cats have even been known to turn on gas fires for extra warmth.

Training a pet kitten

If kittens are to become good pets, they have to be trained by their owner as well as by their mother. You cannot stop cats from jumping on things; it is in their nature. But there are some things they should not be allowed to do. The wise owner lets them know quietly but firmly that these things are forbidden. In this way they grow into gentle and understanding animals. Yet they can never be made very obedient, as can dogs. They will not be pushed into doing things they have no wish to do. They seem to want to make up their own minds. They are intelligent and very independent creatures.

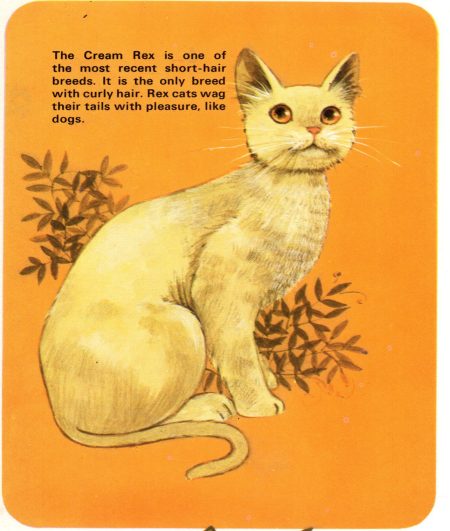

The Cream Rex is one of the most recent short-hair breeds. It is the only breed with curly hair. Rex cats wag their tails with pleasure, like dogs.

Different breeds of cat

Not everyone's idea of a pet cat is a long-haired Tortoiseshell-and-White. Happily there are many different breeds from which to choose.

Some people choose from one of the short-hair breeds, which include the British Blue, the Brown Burmese, the Siamese, the Abyssinian, the Manx. . .

Others prefer the long-hair breeds and choose a Himalayan, a Chinchilla, a Tortoiseshell, a Birman. . .

Each breed has its own special qualities. Tortoiseshell cats, for example, are highly intelligent. A Tortoiseshell kitten will pass a ball to its mother and, if she refuses to play, the kitten will push her claws towards the ball in an attempt to get the mother cat to join in the game.

Legend has it that the tailless Manx came from the Isle of Man. But this is very doubtful. They have long hind legs and walk with a slight hop. They have double coats with a thick, soft undercoat.

The Himalayan, known as Colourpoint in Britain, has the dark face, legs and tail of a Siamese, together with its vivid blue eyes. It is cream all over when first born.

The long-haired Silver tabby. As well as being beautiful, the Silver tabby generally has a good temperament and makes an ideal pet.

The kittens grow up into male or female cats.
Each female cat mates with a male cat.
Her eggs are fertilised and she has kittens.
The kittens grow up into male or female cats.
Each female cat mates with a male cat.
Her eggs are fertilised and she has kittens.
The kittens grow up into male or female cats. . .